THE DEATH OF
LINCOLN

O Captain! my Captain! our fearful trip is done,
The ship has weather'd every rack, the prize we sought is won,
The port is near, the bells I hear, the people all exulting,
While follow eyes the steady keel, the vessel grim and daring;
But O heart! heart! heart!
O the bleeding drops of red,
Where on the deck my Captain lies,
Fallen cold and dead.

Walt Whitman

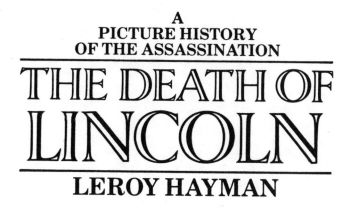

A
**PICTURE HISTORY
OF THE ASSASSINATION**

THE DEATH OF LINCOLN

LEROY HAYMAN

SCHOLASTIC INC.
New York Toronto London Auckland Sydney

ISBN 0-590-44570-7

12 11 10 9   5/9

Printed in the U.S.A.   40

For Fran and Ed, who helped me write this book

Contents

Union Lieutenant General Ulysses S. Grant

Prologue: Appomattox

The day was Palm Sunday, April 9, 1865. The great tragic drama of the Civil War — the War Between the States — was drawing to a close. Begun almost exactly four years before, on April 12, 1861, the conflict had raged from the Atlantic shores to west of the Mississippi River, from Pennsylvania to the Gulf Coast. Now the North, the Union, had triumphed. The South, the Confederacy, was ready to surrender.

The McLean house in the village of Appomattox, Virginia, ninety-five miles west of Richmond, was to be the place where a major Confederate army would acknowledge its defeat. This was not the first home of Wilmer McLean to serve as the setting for an all-important scene of the mighty Civil War drama. In July 1861 his earlier house at Manassas Ridge, Virginia, was caught in the opening crossfire of the first great battle of the war. Thus one McLean house saw the start of the fighting, and another McLean house was witness to the end of the conflict.

General Robert E. Lee, commander of the Army of Northern Virginia, arrived at the McLean house first. Fifty-eight years old, six feet tall, his hair and beard like bright silver, Lee wore a gray Confederate full-dress uniform, with a blue sash across his chest. His boots, spurs, and sword scabbard gleamed in the April sun. Lee was there to accept the conqueror's terms of surrender, but he would do so only with all seriousness and dignity.

Soon Lieutenant General Ulysses S. Grant, head of the Union forces, rode into the McLean yard. An observer described him as wearing a "slouched hat without a cord; common soldier's blouse, unbuttoned, on which, however, the four stars; high boots, mud splashed to the tops; trousers tucked inside, no sword . . ."

Sixteen years younger than Lee and four inches shorter, Grant had stooped shoulders that made him look even smaller than the ramrod-straight Lee. Grant's hair and cropped beard were brown, and an ever-present cigar was clenched between his teeth. Yet in his own way, Grant was equally serious, equally dignified.

Grant had served as a young lieutenant under Lee in the Mexican War, eighteen years before. As the two met in the McLean parlor they exchanged small talk about their service in Mexico. Lee soon led the conversation around to the business at hand: "I suppose, General Grant, that the object of our meeting is fully understood. I asked to see you to ascertain upon what terms you would receive the surrender of my army."

Recalling the exchange of notes which had led to their meeting, Grant had his answer ready: "The terms I propose are those stated substantially in my letter of yesterday — that is, the officers and men surrendered to be paroled and disqualified from taking up arms again until properly exchanged, and all arms, ammunition, and supplies to be delivered up as captured property."

Satisfied with Grant's proposal, Lee nodded in agreement. Grant went on: "I think our correspondence indicated pretty clearly the action that would be taken at our meeting, and I hope it may lead to a general suspension of hostilities and the means of preventing further loss of life."

Seated at a marble-topped table, Grant then wrote out the surrender terms. Lee perched his reading glasses on his nose and closely studied the two pages that Grant had written. At last he smiled, for the first time since entering the McLean house. "This will have a very happy effect on my army."

Lee had a special request to make. Unlike the Union soldiers, Confederate cavalrymen and artillerymen owned their own horses. Could his men keep their mounts in order to do the spring plowing on their farms?

Grant replied with a victor's generosity. He would issue instructions, he said, "to let all the men who claim to own a horse or mule take the animals home with them to work their little farms." Lee answered, "This will have the best possible effect upon the men. It will be gratifying and do much toward conciliating our people."

Lee then asked for food for his Northern prisoners of war and for his own starving troops. Grant directed that twenty-five thousand rations be sent to Lee's army. Lee wrote out and signed an acceptance of Grant's surrender statement. Final details were transacted, and the meeting ended. Lee mounted his

Confederate General Robert E. Lee

horse Traveler, saluted his former foes, and (as one writer put it) "rode off into history."

The end of the war affected all Americans, Union and Confederate, but it had its deepest meaning for one man. More than any other leader, he bore the responsibility for the conduct of the war and the striving for peace. That man was President Abraham Lincoln.

For four tortuous years Mr. Lincoln had seen kin fight against kin, friend ride against friend, each side convinced that it alone was right. For this was the most hellish kind of war — a civil war that divided house and family. And the President was the head of that house, that family. In a very real sense, it was as though his own flesh-and-blood sons were at each other's throats.

President Lincoln knew that for his divided nation the fighting had perhaps stopped, but the war was still on. He was sure that he had years of work ahead of him, laboring to bring peace and reconciliation to both North and South.

Mr. Lincoln was wrong about the part he was to play in peace-making. Before the week was out, for him all wars would be over — forever.

1
DREAM REMEMBERED

On that Palm Sunday, President Lincoln and his wife were aboard the *River Queen,* steaming back to Washington from Virginia. The President had been at City Point and Richmond for several days, noting how Grant had clamped the Confederate forces in his Union vise. Then word had come that Secretary of State William H. Seward had been thrown from his carriage when his horses bolted. The Secretary, age sixty-four, was in sharp pain, his arm and jaw broken.

The *River Queen* docked early in the evening, and Mr. Lincoln hurried to Seward's bedside. Through the iron frame that held his jaw in place, the Secretary gasped: "You are back from Richmond?" "Yes," the President answered, "and I think we are near the end at last." Mr. Lincoln stayed for half an hour, telling in quiet tones the story of the fall of the South's capital city.

War's end

Abraham Lincoln (Alexander Gardner photo)

About nine that night Secretary of War Edwin M. Stanton received a telegram from Grant with the good news of Lee's surrender. Stanton hastened to the White House to inform President Lincoln. The message was heard in heartfelt silence. It was too welcome to inspire ordinary cheers.

By dawn of the next day the happy tidings were all over Washington. Cannon boomed; flags rode merrily on the breeze. All regular work stopped for the day. Washingtonians were in the streets singing and parading.

The President stood at his White House window and watched the frenzied gaiety. To the crowds clustered outside the window he spoke briefly. He asked the Navy Yard band, standing nearby, to play "Dixie," saying, "I have always thought 'Dixie' one of the best tunes I have ever heard."

That day, Monday, Mr. Lincoln sat for a photographic portrait by Alexander Gardner and for the first time since he became President he allowed himself to show a shadow of a smile for the camera. During the last four years the rigors of war leadership had wasted at least thirty-five pounds from his already lean, six-foot four-inch frame. At fifty-six he was not old, but lines of care had cut deep into his sad, bearded face. His eyes mirrored his soul's agony. Perhaps now, with peace, his anguish would abate.

The next day, Tuesday, the President wrote a speech for delivery that evening. A huge audience assembled on the White House lawn to hear him. It was a raucous crowd, made even noisier by several brass bands tooting and thumping. Most of the people had come to hear a boastful, triumphant talk. They were disappointed. Instead of bragging, Mr. Lincoln spoke soberly of the need for restoring self-government to the defeated Southern states, of giving the vote to some of the newly freed slaves. The President was already launched on his mission of "malice toward none, charity for all" expressed in his Second Inaugural Address.

After the speech Mr. and Mrs. Lincoln gathered in the executive mansion's Red Room with a few friends. Among them was Ward Hill Lamon, an old Illinois standby of the Lincolns. At first the conversation, sparked by plump, bustling Mary Lincoln, was chatty and trivial. Then Lamon noted the curious, fateful course that the conversation took.

According to Lamon, the President began discussing dreams. Mrs. Lincoln soon remarked: "Why, you look dreadfully solemn! Do you believe in dreams?"

"I can't say that I do," replied the President, "but I had one the other night which has haunted me ever since. . . ."

Mrs. Lincoln, seeing her husband looking drawn and somehow driven, cried: "You frighten me! What is the matter?"

The President apologized for seeming so obsessed, but said that "somehow the thing has got possession of me." Still frightened, but now even more curious, Mrs. Lincoln pressed him to go on with his tale. Mr. Lincoln began again:

"About ten days ago I retired very late. I had been up waiting for important dispatches from the front. I could not have been long in bed when I fell into a slumber, for I was weary. I soon began to dream. There seemed to be a deathlike stillness about me.

"Then I heard subdued sobs, as if a number of people were weeping. I thought I left my bed and wandered downstairs. There the silence was broken by the same pitiful sobbing, but the mourners were

Mrs. Abraham Lincoln

invisible. I went from room to room; no living person was in sight, but the same mournful sounds of distress met me as I passed along. It was light in all the rooms. Every object was familiar to me. But where were all the people who were grieving as if their hearts would break? I was puzzled and alarmed. What could be the meaning of all this?

"Determined to find the cause of a state of things so mysterious and so shocking, I kept on until I arrived at the East Room, which I entered. There I met with a sickening surprise. Before me was a catafalque, on which rested a corpse wrapped in funeral vestments. Around it were stationed soldiers who were acting as guards. And there was a throng of people, some gazing mournfully upon the corpse, whose face was covered, others weeping pitifully.

"'Who is dead in the White House?' I demanded of one of the soldiers. 'The President,' was his answer; 'he was killed by an assassin!' Then came a loud burst of grief from the crowd, which woke me from my dream. I slept no more that night. And although it was only a dream, I have been strangely annoyed by it ever since."

"That is horrid!" Mrs. Lincoln said. "I wish you had not told me it. I am glad I don't believe in dreams, or I should be in terror from this time forth."

"Well," replied the President, "it is only a dream, Mary. Let us say no more about it, and try to forget it."

Lamon did not set down his notes until many years after Mr. Lincoln's death. But it can be assumed that he was giving a truthful account of the conversation. For even in his waking hours, President Lincoln feared an assassin's blow — and he had good reason.

Mr. Lincoln knew how roundly he was hated in

many circles. In much of the South, men had greeted his Emancipation Proclamation freeing the slaves in the Confederacy with threats to murder him. To be sure, most of these were only hotheaded utterances. But there were still a number of men who, given half a chance, would make good their threat.

In many parts of the North, the President's program of "malice toward none, charity for all" had been received with the same threats. These Northerners had sworn vengeance against the South — and death to anyone who blocked their way. The President's desk held a big envelope labeled "Assassination" — it contained eighty written threats to kill him.

Mr. Lincoln thus always felt death's presence close, yet he knew no way to ward off the fatal blow. He once said: "I do not consider that I have ever accomplished anything without God, and if it is His will that I must die by the hand of an assassin, I must be resigned. I must do my duty as I see it, and leave the rest to God."

And he had told Harriet Beecher Stowe, who wrote *Uncle Tom's Cabin,* "Whichever way the war ends, I have the impression that I shall not last long after it is over."

2
LAST DAY

The fateful day, April 14, 1865, Good Friday, began much as any other day. The President was dressed, out of his bedroom, and on his way to his White House office by 7 A.M. Brushing off the accumulated swarms of hangers-on who tried to trap him with pleas for jobs or special favors, he entered his office.

This was a room in the southeast corner of the second floor of the executive mansion. In the center was a round oak table, used for Cabinet meetings. The President's pigeonhole desk and chair were at the south end of the office. Behind the chair was a velvet bell cord, which he pulled to summon a secretary. An engraved portrait of President Andrew Jackson hung over the mantel.

The President spent an hour at his desk, studying dispatches from the now-quiet battle fronts. Then

Ford's Theatre, Tenth Street, Washington, D.C.

with a sigh of relief he rose and joined his family at breakfast.

Lately there had only been three at the President's table — Mr. and Mrs. Lincoln and their younger son, Tad, age twelve. For the past several months their elder son, Robert, twenty-two, had been on active duty — although well behind the front lines — as a captain on General Grant's staff.

This morning Robert was back with his family, and this was his first chance to talk with his father about what he had seen at Appomattox when Lee surrendered. Tad, spoiled and irrepressible, cut in wherever he could, his cleft palate making some of his talk unintelligible. Two other Lincoln sons had died earlier — Edward in 1850, at four, and Willie in 1862, at twelve. The Lincolns were lavishing an overflow of love on their two remaining sons.

As the President ate his simple breakfast — a single egg, a cup of coffee — Robert put a portrait of General Lee on the table. Mr. Lincoln studied the picture for a long time. Then he said, "It is a good face. It is the face of a noble, brave man. I am glad the war is over."

Back in his office the President received callers: Congressmen, Senators, other government officials. One was Senator John A. J. Cresswell of Maryland, who had helped keep his state in the Union during the war. Cresswell had come to plead the cause of an old friend, a Confederate soldier who was now a Union prisoner: "I know the man acted like a fool, but he is my friend and a good fellow. Let him out, give him to me, and I will be responsible for him."

The President refused the plea with a pointed story: "Cresswell, you make me think of a lot of young folks who once started out Maying. To reach their destination they had to cross a shallow stream,

Tad Lincoln

Robert Lincoln

and did so by means of an old flat boat. When they came to return, they found to their dismay that the old scow had disappeared.

"They were in sore trouble, and thought over all manner of devices for getting over the water, but without avail. After a time one of the boys proposed that each fellow should pick up the girl he liked the best and wade over with her. The masterly proposition was carried out, until all that were left upon the island was a little short chap and a great, long, gothic-built elderly lady.

"Now, Cresswell, you are trying to leave me in the same predicament. You fellows are carrying off one after another until nobody but Jeff Davis [president of the Confederacy, and at the moment in flight] and myself will be left on the island, and then I won't know what to do. How should I feel? How should I look lugging him over? I guess the way to avoid such an embarrassing situation is to let them all out at once."

So the morning went, with requests for releases, pardons, discharges. The President was busy but relaxed. For the moment his mind was free from the sense of doom that had nearly always haunted him in recent years.

Indeed, all of official Washington was relaxed, basking in the sun of peace after four years of war. William H. Crook, Mr. Lincoln's day guard, later wrote: "Those about the President lost somewhat of the feeling, usually present, that his life was not safe. It did not seem possible, now that the war was over . . . after President Lincoln had offered himself a target for Southern bullets in the streets of Richmond and had come out unscathed, there could be any danger."

Between visitors that morning Mr. Lincoln re-

Confederate President Jefferson Davis

membered a task his wife had assigned him. He sent a messenger to Ford's Theatre on Tenth Street, to tell the manager that he and Mrs. Lincoln and friends would attend the performance that evening, and that General Grant would be in the group.

Grant had come with his wife to Washington as soon as his business at Appomattox was done. The General had earlier accepted Mr. Lincoln's invitation to the theatre and to the Cabinet meeting that was now about to begin. It was Grant's first time at a Cabinet session and his first acquaintance with many of the Cabinet members.

The General told Mr. Lincoln privately before the meeting began, however, that he could not attend the theatre that night. He and Mrs. Grant would be on their way to Burlington, New Jersey, to see their daughter at school. But the real truth was that Mrs. Grant disliked Mrs. Lincoln intensely. The First Lady had staged several temper tantrums in front of the General's wife, and Mrs. Grant wanted to face no more of these outbursts.

The Cabinet meeting lasted for three hours — its purpose, in the President's words, to "reanimate the states." Assistant Secretary of State Frederick Seward, son of the Secretary of State, offered several suggestions from his father. Among them: the Treasury Department should take over the Southern customs houses and collect the revenues; the War Department should occupy or destroy all Southern forts; the Navy Department should take over the Confederate navy yards, vessels, and guns; the Post Office Department should re-establish all post offices and mail routes; and so on. In short, the Secretary wanted the U.S. government to take up its tasks again in the South.

And the U.S. government was already doing so.

That very day, as the Cabinet knew, the Stars and Stripes was being raised over Fort Sumter, South Carolina, where the first shots of the Civil War had been fired. General Robert Anderson, who as a major had surrendered the fortress to the South in 1861, was there to see it restored to the United States.

Yet how to deal with the Confederate leaders? Jokingly, Postmaster General William Dennison remarked, "I suppose, Mr. President, that you would not be sorry to have them escape out of the country?"

"Well," said Mr. Lincoln with mock gravity, "I should not be sorry to have them out of the country, but I should be for following them pretty close, to make sure of their going."

Later, as the Cabinet meeting closed, the President returned to the subject, this time seriously: "I hope that there will be no persecution, no bloody work after the war is over. No one need expect me to take any part in hanging or killing these men, even the worst of them. Frighten them out of the country, open the gates, let down the bars, scare them off — enough lives have been lost."

That afternoon Mr. Lincoln took his wife on a long carriage drive — "just ourselves." Along the way he spoke of the next four years and beyond, of the time when they could return to Springfield, Illinois, to his old law practice, and to a new farm on the Sangamon River that flows near Springfield. The President sighed and said, "I have never felt so happy in my life."

It was Mary Lincoln's turn to have a sense of foreboding: "Don't you remember feeling just so before our little boy died?" The "little boy" was Willie, dead just three years.

Mrs. Lincoln's warning must have been on the President's mind as he later walked over to the War

Department with his guard, William Crook. "Crook, do you know, I believe there are men who want to take my life? And I have no doubt they will do it."

"Why do you think so, Mr. President?"

"Other men have been assassinated."

"I hope you are mistaken, Mr. President."

Mr. Lincoln put an end to the discussion, saying, "I have perfect confidence in those who are around me — in every one of you men. I know no one could do it and escape alive. But if it is to be done, it is impossible to prevent it."

At the War Department, the President talked to Secretary of War Stanton about news of the surrender of the remaining Southern armies. Then he asked for someone to accompany him and Mrs. Lincoln to Ford's Theatre that night, explaining that General Grant was unable to come. Could he have Eckert?

Eckert was Major Thomas T. Eckert, chief of the War Department's Telegraph Office, and one of the most physically powerful men in public life. But Stanton said he had other work for Eckert that evening and could not detail him to be at the President's side. In fact, Stanton strongly advised that Mr. Lincoln himself not go to the theatre that night.

At last, however, Stanton assigned a War Department attaché, Major Henry Reed Rathbone, to the task. Rathbone, twenty-eight, was from Albany, New York. His fiancée, Miss Clara Harris, would go too. She was the daughter of U.S. Senator Ira Harris, also from Albany.

At the theatre there was to be, of course, the President's guard. Crook, on the day shift, would be off duty. Taking over from him was to be John F. Parker. A member of the Washington Metropolitan Police Force, Parker had been chosen by Mrs. Lincoln for service at the White House. But Parker,

*Ford's Theatre Program
for April 14, 1865*

whose record was presumably unknown to Mrs. Lincoln, was careless, unreliable, even dishonest. The police board had already tried him fourteen times for violations of orders, inattention to duty, and other transgressions.

After leaving Stanton's office, Mr. Lincoln had second thoughts about that evening. He told Crook, "It has been advertised that we will be there [at Ford's Theatre], and I cannot disappoint the people. Otherwise I would not go. I do not want to go."

This was something of a turnabout, for the President found the theatre a source of relaxation when the going was heavy. Earlier he had written: "Some think I do wrong to go to the opera and the theatre, but it rests me. I love to be alone and yet to be with other people. I want to get this burden off; to change the current of my thoughts. A hearty laugh relieves me, and I seem better able to bear my cross."

The Washington afternoon papers had already come out with the news that the President, Mrs. Lincoln, and General Grant would be attending Ford's Theatre that evening (Grant's withdrawal had come too late to correct the announcement). The play was to be Tom Taylor's popular comedy *Our American Cousin,* with Laura Keene in the leading role of Florence Trenchard, a part she had played more than a thousand times.

The theatre, less than two years old, seated seventeen hundred people. It had a dress circle above the main floor and eight private boxes, four (two upper and two lower) on each side of the stage.

Informed that the Presidential party would attend that night, Harry Clay Ford, the theatre manager, ordered the partition removed between the two upper boxes on the south (stage left) side of the theatre. This created a state box, or President's Box.

President's Box, Ford's Theatre

Ford brought in two U.S. flags on stands and draped another large flag on the balustrade. On the central pillar he placed a gilt-framed engraving of George Washington. As a final touch he ordered an upholstered walnut rocker brought down from his own apartment for the President to sit in.

With the recent news of Lee's surrender — and with the President in attendance — it promised to be a gala evening at Ford's Theatre that night.

The rocker in which Mr. Lincoln sat as he watched the play—and in which he was murdered

3
PREPARATION FOR MURDER

About noon on that Good Friday a pale, handsome young man with a black mustache stopped in the lobby of Ford's Theatre. He was an actor who used Ford's Theatre as his mailing address whenever he was in Washington. While picking up his mail, he learned that the President would attend that evening's performance.

The unexpected news made him tremble with excitement. At last he and his companions would be able to carry out their plans. Their scheme — to be put into action that very night — was to murder Abraham Lincoln! And they planned as well to murder Vice-President Andrew Johnson and Secretary of State Seward.

The young man was John Wilkes Booth, twenty-six. Son of the noted English actor Junius Brutus Booth, John Wilkes was born on a farm north of Baltimore. Asia Booth Clarke, his sister, remembered

John Wilkes Booth

the words of a gypsy fortuneteller who read John Wilkes' palm while he was still a Maryland boy:

"You've a bad hand, the lines all cris-cras! It's full of sorrow — full of trouble — trouble in plenty. You'll break hearts, they'll be nothing to you. You'll make a bad end, and have plenty to love you. You'll have a fast life — short, but a grand one. Young sir, I've never seen a worse hand, and I wish I hadn't seen it, but if I were a girl I'd follow you through the world for your handsome face."

It was only a gypsy's prophecy, bought and paid for with a few pennies. Yet — if Asia was recalling correctly — it proved amazingly accurate.

John Wilkes' two elder brothers, Junius Brutus, Jr., and Edwin, became actors like their father, and Edwin was widely known for his ability in Shakespearian roles. At seventeen John Wilkes took up the family profession. His first performance was as a bit player in Shakespeare's *Richard III.*

Vowing "I must have fame!" his ambition soared beyond his ability. He always confused acting with athletics, substituting leaps and gestures for a real interpretation of the role. Always he was long on action, short on thinking. Yet in his brief career on the stage he had gathered a considerable following.

Maryland, Booth's home state, stayed in the Union during the Civil War, even though it was geographically southern. At first Booth was loyal to the Union cause. In December 1859, sixteen months before the war began, Booth was serving with a militia unit, the Richmond Grays. He was one of the guard that officiated at the hanging of abolitionist John Brown at Charles Town, Virginia. Unlike others who exulted at Brown's execution, Booth wrote his sister, Asia: "Brown was a brave old man. . . ."

Soon, however, Booth shifted his sympathies to

the South. As an actor he attracted his biggest audiences in Southern theatres, where his flamboyant performances were more appreciated than in the North. Yet he never joined the Confederate armed forces. Instead, he slipped back and forth across the front lines many times, and there is some evidence to indicate that he made much money smuggling quinine into the South during those trips.

Booth made acting appearances during the war in New York, Washington, and other Eastern cities. He was in Washington late in 1864 and through the early months of 1865. Once at Ford's Theatre he was playing the part of the villain Pescara in the melodrama *The Apostate* when the President was in his usual box. Booth used the occasion to utter his malevolent lines directly to Mr. Lincoln, gesturing in a threatening way all the while.

"He looks as if he meant that for you," Mr. Lincoln's companion remarked. The President answered, "Well, he does look pretty sharp at me, doesn't he?"

These were no idle gestures. Already a year before Booth had said, "What a glorious opportunity there is for a man to immortalize himself by killing Lincoln!" And there is pictorial proof that Booth and others in the assassination plot were only a few feet from Mr. Lincoln at his Second Inaugural on March 4, 1865. A photograph taken by Alexander Gardner shows the conspirators standing close to the speaker's stand on the steps of the Capitol.

What were the plotters hatching at the moment when Mr. Lincoln was voicing his compassionate message of reconciliation? Booth said later, "What an excellent chance I had to kill the President, if I had wished, on Inauguration Day!"

But the conspirators at first did not plan to kill

Abraham Lincoln. Their original idea was to kidnap him from his box at Ford's Theatre, carry him south to Richmond, and hold him for a giant ransom, including the release of all Confederate prisoners of war. Only gradually, led by Booth, did they evolve the murder scheme. Booth was the unquestioned leader. The others did as they were told, or if they failed to follow orders, did nothing at all.

Booth was set to make his first kidnap attempt on January 18, 1865. In the scheme he enlisted Michael O'Laughlin and Samuel Arnold, old Baltimore friends and Confederate veterans; George Atzerodt, German-born carriage maker from Port Tobacco, Maryland; David Herold, a Washington drug clerk; and John Surratt, Confederate courier, whose mother ran a boardinghouse on H Street in Washington. The plotters met from time to time at Mrs. Surratt's boardinghouse, where each was assigned a part in the abduction.

The schemers were ready at Ford's Theatre on the night of January 18. Only one thing went wrong. Mr. Lincoln changed his plans and did not come to the theatre.

The conspirators scattered, but soon regrouped. This time they had a new member. He was Lewis Paine, a young Confederate veteran, who had known Booth years before. The two had met by chance in Baltimore a month after the first kidnap fiasco, and Booth brought Paine back to Washington. Paine was installed at Mrs. Surratt's boardinghouse under the alias of the Reverend Lewis Wood, Baptist minister.

On March 20 the plotters were again ready for

Mrs. Surratt's boardinghouse, located on H Street, Washington, D.C.

another attempt. They were to kidnap President Lincoln as he rode in his carriage out to the Soldiers' Home at the end of Seventh Street. The President had planned to go there that day to visit the disabled soldiers and to see the afternoon performance of a play put on for them. Only one thing went wrong again. The President changed his plans at the very last moment and did not go.

Again the conspirators scattered. Only Booth, Paine, Atzerodt, and Herold kept in touch. Paine, still calling himself the Reverend Lewis Wood, moved to another boardinghouse, the Herndon House at Ninth and F streets.

Booth groped for an opportunity and a plan of action. He did not find them until on April 14 he learned that Mr. Lincoln was to attend Ford's Theatre that evening. Now it could be done! And this time it would not be kidnapping — it would be murder!

Still trembling with tension, Booth left the theatre lobby that noon. First he went to Howard's Stable on Seventh Street and gave instructions that his own one-eyed horse be put in a shed behind Ford's Theatre. Then at Pumphrey's Livery Stable nearby he hired a little bay mare, asking that it be saddled and ready for him by four. A little after two o'clock he was at Mrs. Surratt's boardinghouse, inquiring for John Surratt. He was told that John was out of town and that Mrs. Surratt was about to leave for Surrattsville, a crossroads settlement twelve miles away. (It had been named for her late husband when he was postmaster there.)

Then Booth did a curious thing — or perhaps only thoughtless or ill-conceived. After drinking brandy at a saloon, he strode into the Kirkwood House and asked the desk clerk if Vice-President Andrew Johnson, who lived there, was in. Told that

Johnson was not, Booth wrote on a card, "Don't wish to disturb you. Are you at home? J. Wilkes Booth." The clerk put the card in the box of Johnson's secretary.

Booth may have previously known Johnson in Nashville when the Vice-President was serving as military governor of Tennessee. Did Booth intend to do away with Johnson himself that afternoon?

Picking up his bay mare at Pumphrey's Livery Stable, Booth tested its speed and went back to his own hotel, the National. There he drank more brandy, wrote a letter, then left the hotel to ride along Pennsylvania Avenue. He saw General and Mrs. Grant in their carriage on their way to the railroad station to board the train for New Jersey. Booth galloped after them and looked closely into the carriage. The word had been that Grant was to be at the theatre that night, but now he was apparently leaving town. Did this mean that Mr. Lincoln had changed his plans as well?

About six o'clock Booth put the bay mare alongside his own horse in the shed behind Ford's Theatre. Edman Spangler, a stagehand, and Joseph "Peanuts" Burroughs, the stage-door keeper, were in charge of the shed. Booth brought a bottle of whiskey for Spangler and Burroughs.

While they were drinking the whiskey, Booth (it is conjectured) slipped up to the President's Box to bore a hole in the door. Through the hole it was possible to observe both the occupants of the box and the action on stage. Booth may have also at this time cut a mortise in the wall opposite the door into the corridor that led from the dress circle to the President's Box. This could be used to anchor a bar to hold the door shut, preventing anyone in the dress circle from entering the corridor.

Michael O'Laughlin

George Atzerodt

Mrs. Mary Surratt

Samuel Arnold

Lewis Paine

Edman Spangler

John Surratt

David Herold

Booth had dinner at his hotel, went up to his room for a brief rest, and left about 8 P.M. On his way out Booth told the desk clerk he ought to be at Ford's Theatre that evening, adding, "there'll be some fine acting there tonight."

At Paine's boardinghouse, Booth huddled with his group to plot out the night's doing. Each took his assignment. Booth was to murder Mr. Lincoln at Ford's Theatre. Paine, guided by Herold, was to slay Secretary Seward in his bedroom at home. Atzerodt was to kill Vice-President Johnson at the Kirkwood House. The four would then meet at the Navy Yard Bridge in Washington, or failing that, at Surrattsville.

Then they would ride south through Virginia, to be hailed as heroes and to be hidden and protected from their pursuers.

4
THE KILLER STRIKES

That Good Friday evening the President and his family sat down to an early dinner. Twelve-year-old Tad was bubbling over at the prospect of going on his own that night to see a children's play at Grover's Theatre. Robert, exhausted by his first taste of army life, retired early to his bedroom. Mr. Lincoln followed him.

"Son," the President said, "I want you to come to the theatre with us tonight."

But Robert begged off. After months of sleeping in a bedroll, he wanted nothing more that night than to enjoy a real bed, complete with linen sheets.

"All right, son," said his father, "run along to bed."

The President still had some official business to care for after dinner. In his office he saw Speaker of the House Schuyler Colfax and Congressman George Ashmun. Ashmun wanted to present one of

Booth fires the fatal shot

the voters from his Massachusetts district, but time was running short. So the President gave him a note that read: "April 14, 1865. Allow Mr. Ashmun & friend to come in at 9 A.M. tomorrow — A. Lincoln." These were the last words the President ever wrote.

With Forbes, the valet and footman, and Burns, the coachman, in attendance, the President and Mrs. Lincoln stepped into their carriage. Two cavalrymen rode behind the vehicle as escorts. Off and away they went, the carriage stopping at Senator Ira Harris' house to pick up Major Rathbone and Clara Harris. The party proceeded to Tenth Street and halted in front of the theatre. The four stepped down from the carriage as passers-by gawked and stared. It wasn't often that people could see the President out for an evening of relaxation.

John F. Parker, the guard assigned to watch over the President that night, was already in the theatre. He had gone to his post outside the President's Box, realized he could not see the play from there, and coolly abandoned it to take a seat in the dress circle. He was watching the play, which had already begun, when the President and his party entered the theatre lobby about 8:25.

Parker came down to the lobby and led the Presidential group to their box. Then he returned to his seat. As Mr. Lincoln entered the box, the performance stopped. Both audience and cast applauded him vigorously, and the orchestra swung into "Hail to the Chief." After some minutes, the play resumed.

Our American Cousin was a comic farce about an uncouth Yankee, Asa Trenchard (played that night by Harry Hawk), who aspires to the title and fortune of his noble English relatives. Mrs. Lincoln, Clara Harris, and Major Rathbone laughed uproariously at the broad humor of the dialogue. The President, however, seemed to be thinking of other matters. Even in the midst of merriment he could not forget his affairs of state.

Mrs. Lincoln was later asked many times what the President's last words were. In her grief and hysteria she seemed to remember at times one remark, at other times another. One version was that she had been sitting so close to her husband that she was impelled to say, apologetically, "What will Miss Harris think of my hanging on to you so?" His answer: "She won't think anything about it."

The other version was that the President had turned to her and said, for no obvious reason, "How I should like to visit Jerusalem sometime!" One or the other of these statements was his very last.

Sometime after nine o'clock Booth rode into the alley behind Ford's Theatre. He was wearing a dark slouch hat, riding clothes, and high spurred boots. He called for Spangler to hold his bay mare, then dismounted and entered the stage door. Spangler turned over the horse's reins to "Peanuts" Burroughs and returned to his backstage duties. Booth wanted to cross the stage behind the scenery but was told that the set extended to the full depth of the stage. So he used a passageway under the stage that led to the front of the theatre and the adjoining Star Saloon, operated by Peter Taltavull.

Ordering whiskey and water instead of his usual brandy, Booth talked to the bartender and the other saloon patrons. Several times he paced nervously from the saloon to the theatre lobby.

About 10:15 Booth stood at the back of the main floor and studied the audience. The play was coming to the end of the second scene of Act III. Booth walked up through the dress circle and into the corridor that led to the President's Box. He closed the door behind him and barred it with a length of wood anchored in the mortise he had cut earlier. Silently he looked through the peephole at the President and the actors beyond.

Onstage the character Mrs. Mountchessington was saying to the "American cousin," Asa Trenchard: "I am aware, Mr. Trenchard, that you are not used to the manners of polite society, and that alone will pardon the impertinence of which you have been guilty." With that she swept offstage, leaving Asa gazing after her.

Asa, thumbs in suspenders, called after her: "Heh, heh. Don't know the manners of good society, eh? Well, I guess I know enough to turn you inside out, old gal — you sock-dologizing old mantrap!"

With the roar of laughter that arose from the audience, Booth pushed open the door of the President's Box and entered it. He drew his weapon, a single-shot, muzzle-loading derringer, .44 caliber, with a ball of Britannia metal a half inch in diameter as the projectile.

Booth fired. The bullet smashed into the President's skull just above the left ear, and stopped a little behind his right eye. Mr. Lincoln inched forward in his chair, then slumped back, conscious no more.

The others in the box were stunned. Then Rathbone leaped upon the assassin. Booth dropped the derringer, drew a large hunting knife, and slashed away at the Major. Rathbone staggered back, blood spurting from a deep wound in his left upper arm. Booth vaulted over the railing, Rathbone frantically grabbing at his clothing. The spur on Booth's right heel caught in the flag draped on the balustrade. He lost balance and landed on his knees on the stage, eleven and a half feet below the box. In the fall, a

Major Henry Reed Rathbone

Booth shouts "Sic Semper Tyrannis" as he flees

bone in his left leg was fractured about two inches above the ankle.

Despite the pain caused by the fracture, Booth leaped to his feet. He struck what he thought was a conquering hero's pose, brandished his knife, and shouted to the audience: *"Sic Semper Tyrannis!"* (Thus always with tyrants! — Brutus' words to the dying Caesar, and the motto of the Commonwealth of Virginia.) Dashing across the stage, he hurried out the back and into the alley. "Peanuts" Burroughs was still holding his horse. Booth struck at the stage-door keeper with the butt of his knife, leaped on his bay mare, and rode swiftly into the night.

5
VIGIL OVER A DYING HERO

For a moment the audience was confused. Many thought that the shot and the man with a knife in his hand leaping from the President's Box to the stage were all part of the play. Then they heard Mrs. Lincoln screaming and Major Rathbone shouting, "Stop that man!"

Dr. Charles Augustus Leale, a young army surgeon, jumped from his seat in the dress circle. He hurried to the door into the corridor leading to the President's Box — the door that Booth had barred moments before he fired the fatal shot. Leale hammered on the door. Rathbone, bleeding from his knife wound, opened it. Ignoring Rathbone's plea for attention, Leale rushed to the President's side.

Mr. Lincoln, slumped over, was supported in his

Mr. Lincoln, dying, is carried to the Petersen house

chair by his wife. She cried out, "Oh, Doctor, is he dead? Can he recover? Will you take charge of him? Do what you can for him. Oh, my dear husband!"

No pulse at the President's wrist could be detected, and he was barely breathing. Laying the President on the floor, Dr. Leale with his pocket knife cut the lifeless man's collar and coat away from the neck and shoulders. He found the bullet wound behind Mr. Lincoln's left ear and freed it of a clot.

With the help of another young army surgeon, Charles Sabin Taft, who soon joined him, Leale began using artificial respiration and mouth-to-mouth breathing methods. The two worked frantically and were rewarded by seeing Mr. Lincoln's breathing become a little more regular and his pulse stirring. Yet both Taft and Leale realized that it was too late. Leale said, "It is impossible for him to recover."

The two surgeons were now augmented by two other doctors from the audience. They were determined, however useless their efforts might prove, to take every step to prolong the President's life. A spoonful of diluted brandy was poured between the President's lips. Laura Keene, the leading lady, sat on the floor with the President's head on her lap and bathed his forehead.

It was plain that Mr. Lincoln must be removed from the floor of the box, but to where? A carriage trip over cobblestoned streets to the White House would surely snuff out his swiftly ebbing life. Across from the theatre was the home of William Petersen, a Swedish-born tailor, who rented extra rooms to lodgers. The doctors ordered Mr. Lincoln to be carried to the Petersen house.

The President was brought into a small (9 by 17 feet) first-floor room and laid slantwise across the narrow bed. (Later it was learned that an actor

Our American Cousin *actress Laura Keene*

Attending surgeon Dr. Charles Augustus Leale

friend of Booth's had formerly rented this room and that Booth had once taken an afternoon nap on this very bed.) Dr. Leale ordered Henry Safford, the lodger who had led them to the room, to begin boiling water in the kitchen and to find any sort of container that would serve as a hot-water bottle to help keep Mr. Lincoln warm.

The four doctors were contemplating their next step when Mrs. Lincoln burst into the room, crying, "Where is my dear husband? Where is he?" She was shunted to a sitting room at the front of the house. There she kept a night-long vigil, alternately sobbing and screaming, and making forays into the room where the President lay.

Meantime, more doctors crowded around the President. Before the night was over, there would be sixteen medical men in attendance, plus Robert Lincoln, Cabinet members, U.S. Senators and Representatives, other government officials, army men, friends of the Lincolns, actors from *Our American Cousin*, and scores of unidentified visitors. In all, more than ninety people were in and out of the death room that night, watching, weeping, praying, crowding close to the dying man.

During the brief time while they were still alone with the President, the four doctors decided that a more complete physical examination was in order. Accordingly, they undressed Mr. Lincoln, beginning with his Brooks Brothers frock coat and his size fourteen boots, custom-made to fit his outsize feet. Knowing that the assassin had slashed Rathbone with a knife, the doctors searched for a knife wound

(Next page) From an engraving by A. H. Ritchie

61

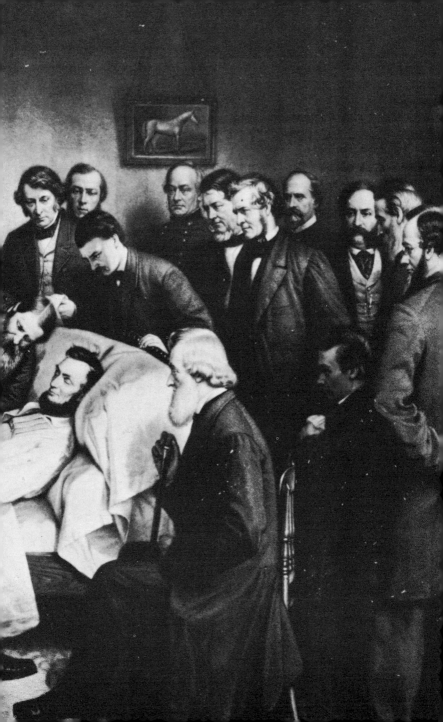

on President Lincoln's body. They found none. The single bullet had done its work well.

What they did find, however, astonished them. The President, divested of his loose-fitting garments, displayed a magnificent frame — smoothly muscled, well-proportioned, lean and strong, with little indication of physical aging. He could have been, Dr. Leale observed, the model for the statue of Moses by Michelangelo.

The Lincoln family physician, Dr. Robert K. Stone, reached the bedside. He was soon joined by Surgeon General Joseph K. Barnes. Mr. Lincoln's limbs were fast losing their body heat, and the cold was extending toward his heart. The doctors applied hot-water bottles and mustard plasters and wrapped their patient in woolen army blankets. They probed the wound, but the bullet was too deep to be extracted. So they sat, awaiting the end. There was nothing more they could do.

Almost at the same moment as Booth fired the fatal shot, another murder was being attempted. Lewis Paine was about to carry out his assignment: kill Secretary of State William H. Seward. At the appointed time, just after 10 P.M., Paine (on Booth's one-eyed mount) and David Herold rode up to Seward's house in Lafayette Square, near the White House. Herold held the horses as Paine entered the house.

Seward, still in constant pain from his injuries, lay in an upstairs bedroom. Watching over him were his daughter Fanny and a soldier-nurse, George T. Robinson. One son, Major Augustus Seward, had gone to bed early. He was scheduled to take over the watch from Fanny and Robinson at 11 P.M. The Secretary's other son, Frederick (the Assistant Secretary of State), was awake in his own room.

Fanny Seward and Secretary of State William H. Seward

Hearing heavy footsteps on the stairs, Robinson said to Fanny, "Wouldn't you think that a person would be more quiet coming up to a sickroom?" Expecting no danger, they were merely annoyed, not alarmed. Frederick too heard the heavy tread and went to see who it was. It was Paine, with a small package in his hand. The package, Paine told Frederick, was medicine from Seward's doctor, and he was under orders to deliver it to the Secretary personally.

Frederick protested that his father was asleep and too ill, besides, to take delivery of any package. The two argued for a time. Suddenly Paine drew his revolver, aimed it at Frederick, and pulled the trigger. The gun failed to go off. Paine quickly used it as a hammer to beat Frederick savagely about the head.

Then, knife in hand, Paine burst into the sickroom. He cut down Robinson with a knife thrust and beat Fanny away with his fists. Then he leaped onto the bed and slashed viciously at Seward's face and neck. Only the iron brace around Seward's jaw saved his life.

Robinson rallied and came to the Secretary's defense. Grappling, the soldier-nurse and the would-be assassin rolled into the corridor. Major Augustus, awakened by the tumult, came out and mistakenly grabbed Robinson. "For God's sakes, Major," Robinson cried, "let go of me and take the knife out of his hand — and cut his throat!"

Freeing himself from Robinson's grasp, Paine struck at the Major with his knife. Then he ran down the stairs and out the front door, shouting "I am mad! I am mad!"

Outside, Paine looked for Herold and for his one-eyed horse. He found the horse tied to a tree, but Herold had vanished. Paine mounted and slowly rode off. Unfamiliar with Washington, he tried to remember where he was supposed to go. Without Herold, his guide, he was lost.

Meantime, Robinson and Major Augustus lifted Seward back into bed and removed the bloody linens and nightclothes. Despite his combined injuries, the Secretary clung strongly to life. He told his son, "I am not dead, send for a surgeon, send for the police, close the house."

Another important person was sent for as well. He was Secretary of War Stanton, who lived just across the square — and who had visited Seward only moments before Paine made his near-fatal attack. Stanton was preparing for bed when the word came. He hurried across the square to find Seward brutally slashed, with a doctor attempting to stanch the flow of blood. It was at that moment that Stanton heard even more terrible news: that Mr. Lincoln was an assassin's victim, his life swiftly draining away.

Stanton knew what he had to do — take command of the situation. He sped to the Petersen house on Tenth Street and set up a post next to the room where the President lay dying. He called for the Assistant Secretary of War, Charles A. Dana, who lived next door and enlisted the help of a government clerk, James Tanner. Tanner took shorthand notes as Stanton questioned witnesses and rapped out a constant stream of orders.

Stanton's task was huge; everything had to be done at once. The whole nation had to be told of the tragedy. Statements had to be taken from witnesses before they drifted away. The killer had to be identified — which he soon was. The order went out: Find John Wilkes Booth, "twenty-five years old [he was actually twenty-six], five feet eight inches tall, dark hair and mustache. Use all efforts to secure him."

Roadblocks were set up on routes to Maryland. All passenger trains and Potomac River ships heading south were stopped and searched. The countryside surrounding Washington was mapped out for search as soon as it was light.

Stanton, known to be a merciless man, was brutally efficient that night. Dr. Leale recalled his treatment of Mary Lincoln:

"During the night Mrs. Lincoln came frequently from the adjoining room accompanied by a lady friend. At one time Mrs. Lincoln exclaimed sobbing bitterly, 'Oh! That my little Taddy might see his father before he died!' While Mrs. Lincoln sat on a chair by the side of the bed with her face to her husband's, his breathing became very stertorous and the loud unnatural noise frightened her. She sprang up suddenly with a piercing cry and fell fainting to the floor. Secretary Stanton, hearing her cry, came in from the adjoining room and with raised arms called out loudly, 'Take that woman out and do not let her in again!'"

One of Stanton's messages was to Vice-President Andrew Johnson, telling him to be prepared to take the Presidential oath of office. Johnson did not know at the time that he also had been marked for assassination. Nor did he know that his intended killer was George Atzerodt, who had flubbed his assignment. A weak-willed alcoholic, Atzerodt had panicked at the prospect of killing a high government official. Instead, Atzerodt had thrown his knife away and got thoroughly drunk.

Now, sometime after midnight, Johnson was determined to pay his last respects to the President. He and Mr. Lincoln had never been close, and Mrs. Lincoln — for no reason that he could understand — had singled him out as one of her special foes.

One of many reward posters

President Andrew Johnson (1865-69)

Johnson came to the President's bedside and stood for a few minutes in silence. Then, as Mrs. Lincoln was about to make one of her periodic visits to her dying husband, Johnson was quickly hustled out of the room. Returning to his hotel, Johnson paced the floor the rest of the night. Over and over again he repeated, "They shall suffer for this! They shall suffer for this!"

As morning came the President began to moan. His breathing became quick and shallow, his skin icy cold. Surgeon General Barnes asked that Mrs. Lincoln be brought in. Robert Lincoln was at the bedside sobbing. Mrs. Lincoln looked at her dying husband and weeping son, and unable to bear the agony, fled the room.

Dr. Leale watched the President struggle for breath. He saw Mr. Lincoln's chest rise, fall, then rise no more. John Hay, the President's personal secretary, later wrote: "A look of unspeakable peace came over his worn features. Stanton broke the silence by saying, 'Now he belongs to the ages.' "

It was 7:22 A.M., April 15, 1865. Abraham Lincoln, sixteenth President of the United States of America, was dead.

Mourning arch over railroad tracks at Sing Sing, N. Y.

6
HOME FOREVER

The President and Mrs. Lincoln had been at City Point and Richmond, Virginia, for several days before returning to Washington on that last Sunday of the President's life. One day they had gone driving along the James River outside City Point. The war was nearing its end, and Mr. Lincoln was cheerful. As they passed an old country church, the President had the driver stop, and husband and wife strolled in the churchyard.

On the graves were flowering jonquils, iris, arbutus; the trees and shrubs were alive with new green leaves. The scene was eternally peaceful. Moved by the lovely stillness, Mr. Lincoln said, "Mary, you are younger than myself. You will survive me. When I am gone, lay my remains in some quiet place like this."

That day Mary Lincoln had put off thinking about the President's request. She felt that it would be years before she would have to consider her husband's last resting place, and her own. Yet she kept it in the back of her mind. For Mary Lincoln, whatever may have been wrong with her (she was judged mentally incompetent after the President's death), was always in love with her husband. She knew that wherever Mr. Lincoln was buried, she wanted, when her time came, to be beside him.

Now, only scant days after he had told her of his wishes, Mrs. Lincoln had to decide where his grave was to be. Overcoming for the moment her anguish and her grief, she was firm in denying bids by New York City and Washington to provide a burial place. In one of those places, the President would have to lie in majestic solitude, without his wife. Instead she chose Springfield, Illinois, where young Abe Lincoln had settled twenty-eight years before, and where they had been married in 1842. She wanted to return to the scene of their happiest days, their days of joy and fulfillment.

But Mary Lincoln also realized that hers was to be no private grief. She had to share her mourning with the whole nation. For people everywhere in the North and South were immeasurably saddened by the President's tragic death. The North's joy over the end of the Civil War was turned to sorrow by the assassination. The South, already brought low by its defeat, could not rejoice in the murder. Many Southerners had hated Mr. Lincoln as President of the Union and leader of the foe, but they did not hate him as a man. When the man was slain, their hearts went out to his widow and sons and to his memory.

To be sure, there were those in both the North and the South who secretly exulted at the crime. Some Northerners had despised Mr. Lincoln for his compassion toward the enemy; they demanded total defeat, total subjugation. Some Southerners were furious at the President because he had freed the Negroes; to them, any such opponent of slavery was base and contemptuous.

For the moment, however, those who still hated the slain Abraham Lincoln were lying low. On that Easter Saturday, news of the tragedy was swiftly telegraphed across the country. Black-bordered newspapers headlined the story of the assassination. The public immediately expressed their sorrow in countless ways — flags at half-mast, crapes and mourning bands worn on clothing, all cheer and celebration canceled. To many who had never seen the President in life the loss was as genuine as the passing of their own father.

In Washington the funeral plans were projected on a grand scale. In charge of local preparations was George A. Harrington, Assistant Secretary of the Treasury. At once he ordered an elaborate catafalque be set up in the East Room of the White House. It was ready by Monday night, April 17, and the President in his coffin was quietly brought down from a guest room.

The East Room, on the east side of the White House, was 40 by 80 feet; its ceiling was 22 feet high. The catafalque consisted of posts supporting an arched canopy, under which lay a dais, 11 feet long and 3 feet high. The coffin rested on this dais. The catafalque was swathed in black alpaca, velvet, and satin, arranged in complicated festoons and rosettes. Mirrors in the East Room were framed in black cloth and the glass covered with white cloth. Black streamers hung from the cornices. Window drapes were drawn. The whole room presented an appearance of unrelieved sadness.

The coffin itself was walnut, covered with black

Mr. Lincoln's coffin

broadcloth and lined with white satin. Under the walnut was a heavy lining of lead. Four silver handles were on each side, and on the lid was a silver plate with the simple inscription:

Abraham Lincoln
16th President of the United States
Born February 12, 1809
Died April 15, 1865

Early Tuesday morning a long line of people began forming in front of the White House, ready to take their last look at their beloved President. At 9:30 they began filing through the South Portico to the East Room. That day at least twenty-five thousand saw the catafalque with its mournful burden. Among them was a group of disabled soldiers from nearby military hospitals. Heavily bandaged, many on crutches or canes, they passed in silence by the bier of their slain commander in chief.

About 7:30 P.M. the East Room doors were shut, and carpenters began preparing for the next day's funeral service. They built tiers of steps all around the room so that all invited guests could have a clear view of the ceremonies. Harrington divided the tiers into sections, each with a card showing the name of the group to occupy that section.

The funeral morning, Wednesday, April 19, dawned warm and bright. The magnolias were just coming into bloom in Washington. At sunrise, cannon boomed in the forts near the city and bells tolled in the churches and firehouses. Washingtonians and thousands of visitors were ready to pay a "last full measure of devotion."

About six hundred invitation cards had been issued for admittance to the East Room service. The principal guest was the new President, Andrew Johnson, who had been sworn in about three hours after Mr. Lincoln died. General Grant was allowed to take a solitary place at the head of the coffin; he wept throughout the service. Other guests included members of the U.S. Supreme Court, the Cabinet, and Congress.

Robert and Tad Lincoln were present, but Mary Lincoln could not face the ordeal. She spent the day confined to her bed. Secretary of State Seward, still suffering greatly from his recent injuries and new wounds, was unable to come. A large Illinois delegation was in attendance.

The service began as the Rev. Charles A. Hall read from the Episcopal burial service: "I am the Resurrection and the Life. . . ." Then Methodist Bishop Matthew Simpson recited a long eulogy, ending with the Lord's Prayer: "Our Father which art in Heaven . . ." The Lincoln family pastor, the Rev. Phineas D. Gurley, a Presbyterian, gave the long funeral sermon, dwelling on this "mysterious and most afflicting visitation." The service closed as Chaplain of the Senate Edwin H. Gray, a Baptist, offered a long prayer ending with "God of Justice and Avenger of the Nation's wrong, let the work of treason cease, and let the guilty perpetrators of this horrible crime be arrested and brought to justice. . . ."

Ward Hill Lamon was in charge of the funeral procession that led from the White House to the Capitol, where the President was to lie in state. At the head of the procession, in front of the hearse, was a detachment of Negro soldiers. Behind the hearse came Mr. Lincoln's horse, saddled but riderless, with the President's boots reversed in the stir-

Mourners march from White House to Capitol

rups (following an old military custom). Then came Robert and Tad Lincoln in a carriage. After them followed a host of mourners, low- and high-ranking, military and civilian. Notable in the line was a contingent of four thousand Negro men, wearing high silk hats and white gloves, holding hands as they marched.

Uncounted thousands thronged the sidewalks, and other viewers crowded into windows and on roofs along the route. Accompanied by dirges and drumbeats from thirty marching bands spaced along the way, the procession moved slowly and with majestic solemnity. The hearse reached the Capitol at 3:30 P.M., and pallbearers carried the coffin to another catafalque beneath the Rotunda. A huge crowd listened as Dr. Gurley intoned a sad invocation: ". . . the dust returns to the earth as it was and the Spirit unto God Who gave it. . . ." Then all withdrew, leaving the coffin in charge of the Guard of Honor.

The next morning, Thursday, the public was admitted at eight. All day long people filed past the coffin in a steady line. All were sad; many wept openly. They departed through the east door and down the long stone staircase, past the place where Mr. Lincoln had twice taken the oath as President. It was Washington's last chance to see its beloved leader.

On Friday morning, April 21, Mr. Lincoln began his long journey home. After a prayer by Dr. Gurley the coffin was taken from the Capitol to the railroad depot and placed aboard a funeral car. It was one of nine cars, plus an engine, that made up the funeral train. There was also a pilot engine that cleared the track in front of the funeral train. The funeral car itself was second from the end.

Mr. Lincoln's coffin was not the only one in the

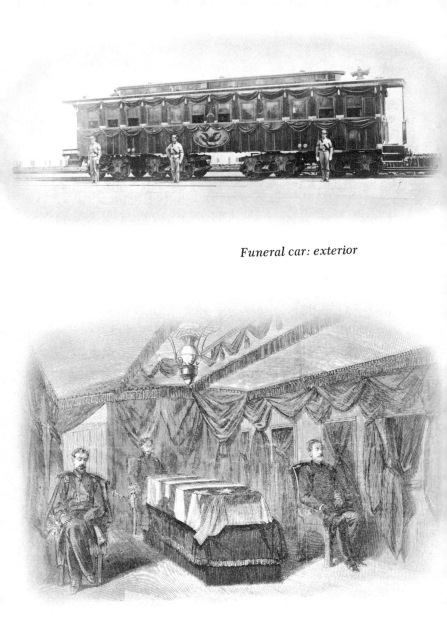

Funeral car: exterior

Funeral car: interior

car. It was decided that the coffin of Willie, his deceased son, would accompany that of his father to the final resting place. Dead since 1862, Willie had been interred in a vault in Georgetown's Oak Hill Cemetery. Now the two would go home together.

Three hundred people were to ride in the funeral train back to Springfield. They included Lincoln relatives (but not the immediate family), friends, government officials, clergy, and even Thomas Pendel, the White House doorkeeper, who was a special friend of Tad's.

The route that the train was to follow was an already-historic one. It included almost every city that President-elect Lincoln had stopped at on his journey from Springfield to Washington, bound for the Inauguration on March 4, 1861. Only Cincinnati was omitted — it was too far out of the way. The seventeen-hundred-mile itinerary included stops at Baltimore, Harrisburg, Philadelphia, New York, Albany, Buffalo, Columbus, Indianapolis, Chicago, and at the end, Springfield.

Each city vied with the others in its expression of lament and sorrow. Huge crowds turned out to pay homage to the dead President, even though the stop was in the dead of night or in pouring rain. In each city the coffin was displayed in an elaborate setting; in Harrisburg, for example, the catafalque was in the State House of Representatives. There, mourners filed past the bier in endless succession. There were also "farewell parades" to and from the railroad depots.

And always, in order to maintain its schedule, the funeral train had to depart while long lines of mourners were still awaiting their chance to say good-bye. Even at communities where the funeral train passed through without halting, people crowded along the railroad tracks and waved a forlorn farewell.

On Wednesday, May 3, Mr. Lincoln and Willie came home to Springfield. Abraham Lincoln had departed the Illinois state capital more than four years before. In saying farewell he had opened his heart to those gathered around him at the railroad station:

"My friends, no one not in my situation can appreciate my feelings of sadness at this parting. To this place, and the kindness of these people, I owe everything. Here I have lived a quarter of a century, and have passed from a young to an old man. Here my children have been born, and one is buried. I now leave, not knowing when, or whether ever, I may return. . . ."

Each city along the funeral train route had been passionate in its demonstrations of sorrow, but Springfield outdid all the others. The President lay in state in the Hall of Representatives in the State House, where he had delivered his epochal "House Divided" speech in 1858. The outside of the State House was adorned with black and white mourning wrappings, rosettes, and streamers in wagonload quantities. Inside, the catafalque, twenty-four feet high, was more elaborate than the one in the White House.

And the whole town was equally demonstrative in its outpouring of grief. Everywhere one looked, there was some sign or show that here people were mourning one of their own, a native son who had died a martyr's death.

The mourning was expressed in curious ways. On that May 3 at least five thousand people came to the Lincoln home, now rented to the Tiltons. They wanted to see everything associated with Mr. Lincoln, and they stripped the garden for floral souve-

Mr. Lincoln's tomb: Oak Ridge Cemetery Springfield, Ill.

nirs, even chipping paint from the house and prying bricks from the walls. The visitors could have been accused of being only morbid souvenir hunters. Yet perhaps each one only wanted to carry away a little remembrance of Mr. Lincoln for himself.

Visitors also had a look at the First Presbyterian Church, where the Lincoln family worshipped, Mr. Lincoln's law office and his bank, even the barber shop where Mr. Lincoln paid fifteen cents for a haircut. They wandered around town as if trying to see Springfield through Mr. Lincoln's eyes.

Starting at 10 A.M. on May 3, mourners passed by Mr. Lincoln's bier in the State House for a full twenty-four hours. Then final burial preparations were made. The coffin was closed, and pallbearers carried it to the waiting hearse. The long, slow journey to Oak Ridge Cemetery, two miles away, began. Thousands and thousands followed the hearse on foot, so many that some had not yet reached the graveyard by the time the service was over.

It was estimated that seventy-five thousand people crowded into the cemetery for the last rites. These began as the Reverend A. C. Hubbard read Mr. Lincoln's Second Inaugural Address, full of compassion and mercy: "with malice toward none; with charity for all. . . ." Bishop Simpson gave the funeral oration, saying: "He made all men feel a sense of himself — a recognition of individuality — a self-relying power. They saw in him a man who they believed would do what is right, regardless of all consequences." Dr. Gurley offered the benediction, and a last hymn was sung.

The gates of the tomb swung shut, and the crowd slowly scattered. It was May 4, 1865. Twenty days before, the President had been alive. Now he had reached his final resting place.

Dr. Samuel Mudd's home: Bryantown, Maryland

7
FLIGHT INTO DARKNESS

On that fatal night of April 14, 1865, Booth, astride his rented bay mare, rode swiftly from the alley behind Ford's Theatre. He galloped along F Street, around the Capitol to Pennsylvania Avenue, and over to the Navy Yard Bridge that spans the Anacostia River.

The bridge sentry was unaware that a horrible crime had just been committed. But he was under standing orders to let no one cross the bridge after 9 P.M. without official permission. However, Booth, giving his real name, pleaded that he lived near Beantown, Maryland. He had been in Washington that day on business, he said, and had not known of the nine o'clock rule. The sentry let him pass.

A few minutes later a man calling himself Smith gave much the same story to the sentry. He too was allowed to cross the bridge. It is believed that this second man was David Herold. He was the conspirator who had accompanied Lewis Paine on his mission to murder Secretary of State Seward. But Herold had fled before Paine rushed out of the Seward mansion, the murder mission bungled. At any rate, Booth and Herold met somewhere in the Maryland countryside before midnight.

The two stopped at a tavern in Surrattsville, where they picked up carbines, whiskey, and a field glass. According to John Lloyd, the tavern-keeper, these had been left for them by Mrs. Surratt on Friday. Booth may have given the objects to her when he called at the boardinghouse to ask for her son John.

About 4 A.M. on the morning that Mr. Lincoln died, Booth and Herold rode up to the home of Dr. Samuel A. Mudd, near Bryantown, Maryland. Dr. Mudd was known to be a warm Southern supporter. Booth and the doctor knew each other, but Dr. Mudd claimed later that he did not recognize Booth on this visit.

The doctor splinted Booth's broken leg and put him to bed for several hours. That afternoon Herold and Booth continued on their flight. They followed a trail through Zekiah Swamp which led eventually to the Potomac River. Across the river lay Virginia — and, they hoped, safety.

At Brice's Chapel they persuaded a Negro, Oswald Swann, to take them to the house of Samuel Cox. They had been told earlier that Cox would help them along on their journey. News of the President's assassination had already reached Cox, and he was afraid to let Booth and Herold stay at his home. He fed the two and hid them in the nearby woods. Then Cox sent his son to tell Thomas Jones, his foster brother, of his "visitors."

Jones was a zealous believer in the Southern

cause. He said to Cox, "Sam, I will see what I can do, but the odds are against me. I must see these men."

Led to Booth, Jones later described the scene:

"He was lying on the ground with his head supported on his hand. His carbine, pistols and knife were close beside him. A blanket was partly drawn over him. His slouch hat and crutch were lying by him. He was exceedingly pale and his features bore the evident traces of suffering. I have seldom seen a more strikingly handsome man.

"No sooner had I seen him in his helpless and suffering condition than I gave my whole mind to the problem of how to get him across the river. . . . I promised to bring him food every day, and to get him across the river just as soon as it would not be suicidal to make the attempt.

"He said he knew the Government would use every means in its power to secure his capture. 'But,' he added . . .'John Wilkes Booth will never be taken alive.' He seemed very desirous to know what the world thought of his deed, and asked me to bring him some newspapers. . . ."

Each day for the next five days Jones brought food and papers to the two fugitives. Their horses, which couldn't be ferried across the Potomac, might give away their hiding place to close-riding pursuers, so the horses were shot.

On one of these days Jones went into Port Tobacco to learn what he could of the search for Booth. At the bar in Brawner's Tavern a detective named Williams informed him that $100,000 would be paid for information leading to Booth's capture.

"That's an awful lot of money," said Jones. "If money will do it, that ought to be enough." No amount of money was enough to tempt Jones.

On Monday, April 17, the day after Booth and

Brawner's Tavern, where Jones heard offer of $100,000 for Booth's capture

Thomas Jones

Herold came under Jones' protection, Michael O'Laughlin surrendered in Baltimore. He confessed that he had been part of the earlier scheme to kidnap the President, but he swore he had not been in on the murder. The same day, Samuel Arnold was arrested in Fortress Monroe, Virginia. He admitted to the same degree of involvement in the crime as O'Laughlin.

Also picked up that same day was Edman Spangler, the Ford's Theatre stagehand. He had become caught up in the web of murder by holding Booth's horse in the theatre alley on the night of the murder.

That night the police swooped down on Mrs. Surratt's boardinghouse. Louis Weichmann, one of the boarders, had earlier accused her son John Surratt of being one of the plotters in the kidnap scheme. The police, however, had paid no attention at the time to Weichmann's story of the abduction plot.

Now the police were ready to arrest Mrs. Surratt and her daughter Annie. While they were waiting for the two to gather personal articles for a jail stay, someone knocked on the door. It was Lewis Paine, dressed as a laborer and with a pick over his shoulder.

Paine had been hiding in a treetop in the woods for three days since fleeing the Seward house. He had come back to Mrs. Surratt's boardinghouse, seeking his fellow plotters — the only friends he had in Washington. He had a story evidently concocted for just such an emergency as this. It was that he had been hired to dig a ditch for Mrs. Surratt the next morning and had come by that evening to get instructions.

But Mrs. Surratt had poor eyesight. She failed to recognize Paine even though he had lived in her boardinghouse recently for a time under the alias of the Rev. Lewis Wood. Turning to the police, she said she did not know Paine, and wanted protection from such an obvious liar. The police arrested Paine on general suspicion. Only later was he identified as the man who had attacked Secretary Seward.

On Thursday, April 20, the police arrested George Atzerodt in Rockville, Maryland. Atzerodt, assigned to slay Vice-President Andrew Johnson, had panicked and never went near his intended victim. However, he had been one of the plotters from the very first, and was thus liable to arrest and trial.

The next day Dr. Samuel Mudd was arrested. He was closely questioned but allowed to stay at his farm home over the weekend. Then on Monday, April 24, he was taken to Washington and jailed.

Meantime, Booth and Herold still eluded their pursuers. In hiding, Booth still managed to find time to make occasional entries in his diary. His entry for Friday, April 21, tells much about his own concept of his "mission":

"After being hunted like a dog through swamps and woods, and last night being chased by gun boats until I was forced to return, wet, cold, and starving, with every man's hand against me, I am here in despair. And why? For doing what Brutus was honored for, what made William Tell a Hero. And yet I for striking down an even greater tyrant than they ever knew, am looked upon as a common cutthroat. My act was purer than either of theirs. . . . I struck for my country, and her alone. A people ground beneath this tyranny prayed for this end, and yet now see the cold hands they extend to me. God cannot pardon me if I have done wrong; yet I cannot see any wrong, except in serving a degenerate people. . . . For my country I have given up all that makes life sweet

Paine is captured at Mrs. Surratt's boardinghouse

and holy, brought misery upon my family, and am sure there is no pardon for me in the heavens, since man condemns me so. . . . God, try to forgive me and bless my mother. . . . I have . . . almost a mind to return to Washington, and in a measure clear my name, which I feel I can do."

Booth was half out of his mind with exhaustion, hunger, and the pain of his broken leg. But were he well and able, he still would have made much the same entry in his diary. For Booth was absolutely convinced that he was right in slaying Mr. Lincoln. He was certain sure that he had acted in the South's best interest — whether Southerners knew it or not. And he pitied himself for the South's "ingratitude."

The day Booth wrote this diary entry was the day that the President's funeral train left Washington on its roundabout journey to Springfield. That same day Thomas Jones learned that the search for Booth would be shifted to another area in the capital countryside. This would be the best time for the two fugitives to break for the Potomac crossing.

That night Jones led Booth and Herold three miles to the river and to a rowboat he had secreted below Dent's Meadow. Giving them directions and bidding them good-bye, Jones would accept eighteen dollars in payment for the rowboat and nothing more for all his help.

Herold rowed for long hours until they believed they had crossed the Potomac and were in the mouth of Machodoc Creek on the Virginia side. But when dawn broke, they realized that they were still on the Maryland side. The incoming ocean tide had carried them up the river into the mouth of Nanjemoy Creek. They waited all day in the boat and that night made a successful river crossing, coming ashore on the banks of Gambo Creek.

They soon found Thomas Harbin, a friendly guide. He passed them along to Dr. Richard Stewart, another who was known for his Confederate loyalty. The doctor sent out food to the two fugitives, but refused to treat Booth, much less see him. Booth, angered by this indifference, left a note for Dr. Stewart:

> Forgive me, but I have some little pride. I hate to blame you for your want of hospitality, you know your own affairs. I was sick and tired, with a broken leg, in need of medical advice. I would not have turned a dog away from my door in such a condition. However, you were kind enough to give me something to eat for which I thank you, and because of the manner in which it was bestowed I feel bound to pay for it. . . . Be kind enough to accept the enclosed $5, though hard to spare, for what we have received.
>
> Yours respectfully,
> Stranger

Rereading the note before leaving it, Booth modified his haughty tone just a little. He scratched out the "$5" and substituted "$2.50." But he still wallowed in self-pity.

Hidden under straw in a wagon, Booth and Herold were transported to Port Conway on the Rappahannock River. Also waiting for the ferry to take them across the three-hundred-yard stream were three Confederate army officers, William J. Jett, A. S. Bainbridge, and M. B. Ruggles, who were on their way home. Herold could not contain the secret; he told the officers who he and Booth were. Booth was frightened by Herold's blabbing, but the officers promised to help them.

Across the Rappahannock, the officers tried to lodge Booth and Herold for the night at the home of Randolph Peyton, a friend of Jett's. But Peyton was away from home. His sisters, while cordial, would not consider putting up male strangers for the night. Nearby, however, lived a man named Richard Garrett, another friend of Jett's. The Confederate officers were sure he would help.

Jett introduced Booth as "John W. Boyd" (to account for the initials tattooed on the back of Booth's right hand), a Confederate soldier wounded at Petersburg. Seeing Booth's "wounds," Garrett was eager to put him up for a little time. Herold stayed behind, and was later presented as Davey, "Boyd's" younger brother.

Garrett's family included his wife and sons, Jack and William, two young daughters, and Mrs. Garrett's sister, Miss Holloway. All were friendly to Booth, especially Miss Holloway, a young schoolteacher, who was taken by his charm.

The Confederate officers then said good-bye to the Garretts and to Booth and Herold. But they were soon back with bad news. They had just heard that a band of federal soldiers had crossed the Rappahannock at Port Royal. Booth and Herold, thoroughly frightened, scurried out of the Garrett house and hid in the woods. The two heard the troops ride by on their way to Bowling Green. What they didn't know was that the Rapphannock ferryman had reported taking a man on a crutch and his companion across the river. The federal troops were sure they were hot on the trail of the right men.

After a time Booth and Herold returned to the Garrett house. Booth tried to explain their panicky flight to the woods by saying that they'd had "trouble" in Maryland and that the soldiers might be after them. They now asked Garrett to rent them horses—they wanted to ride to Guinea Station, eleven miles away, where they could board the train for Richmond.

But Garrett became wary. He had not yet heard the assassination details, but he was suspicious. Were these two Confederate veterans—or were they something else? He told Booth and Herold he would furnish them horses next morning; it was already too late that night.

Booth in turn was taking no chances. He asked if he and his "brother" could sleep in the barn. Garrett told them to make their beds in an old tobacco drying shed on his property. And when they retired, Garrett instructed his sons to put a lock on the shed door and themselves to sleep — with one eye open — in the corn cribs close by.

Whoever these strangers were, they were not going to steal *his* horses during the night. But Garrett did not know that a different fate awaited his now unwelcome guests.

Sergeant Boston Corbett (left) and Lieutenant L.P. Doherty

8
DEATH FOR THE SLAYER

The federal soldiers who had ridden past the Garrett house were still hot in pursuit of their quarry. They found Jett holed up in a room in a Bowling Green hotel and forced him to reveal the whereabouts of Booth and Herold. The soldiers swiftly backtracked to the Garrett farm and surrounded the tobacco barn.

L. P. Baker, a detective with the troops, shouted an ultimatum: unless the two were out within five minutes, soldiers would set fire to the barn!

Booth shouted back, "Who are you? What do you want? Whom do you want?"

"We want you, and we know who you are. Give up your arms and come out," replied Baker.

Booth offered to bargain: "Let us have a little time to consider it."

After ten or fifteen minutes of such palavering, Booth made another offer: "Captain, I know you to be a brave man and I believe you to be honorable. I am a cripple. I have got but one leg. If you will withdraw your men in line one hundred yards from the door, I will come out and fight you."

This proposal, and another like it, was refused. Booth, still the actor, said, "Well, my brave boys, prepare a stretcher for me."

The talk died down for a time. Then Booth suddenly called out, "There's a man in here wants to come out."

Baker called back, "Very well, let him hand his arms out and come out." The soldiers could hear Booth saying to Herold, "You damned coward, will you leave now? Go, go; I would not have you stay with me."

Herold opened the barn door, put his hands out in front of him, and was quickly led away. At once he was wild in protesting his innocence, but he was told to be silent or be gagged.

Lieutenant L. P. Doherty, commander of the federal force, then made up his mind as to his next step. He ordered a soldier to set fire to a straw rope and throw it on a pile of hay inside the barn. Soon the whole barn was ablaze. Booth was insanely determined to have his last moment of glory. He hopped around just inside the barn door, crutch under one arm, trying to aim his carbine with his other arm.

Secretary of War Stanton had issued strict orders to bring the assassin back alive. The soldiers were ready to obey those orders — all except one. He was Sergeant Boston Corbett. His fellow troopers knew Corbett to be a religious fanatic, and some considered him quite mad.

Seeing Booth through the cracks in the barn wall, Corbett suddenly fired his pistol. The bullet hit Booth in the back of the head — in just about the same place as President Lincoln's fatal wound had been. Asked later why he had fired against orders, Corbett pointed his finger at the sky and said, "God Almighty directed me." His questioner replied, "Well, I guess He did or you couldn't have hit him through that crack in the barn."

As soon as Booth fell, soldiers rushed in and carried him out of the burning barn. The dying man was brought to the porch of the Garrett house. In barely audible tones he gasped out, "Tell my mother I died for my country . . . and I did what I thought was the best." Later he whispered, "Did Jett betray me?"

Booth then asked to have his hands lifted so he could see them. Looking at his hands, he mumbled, "Useless. Useless." These were his last words. He died just as the sun rose on the morning of Wednesday, April 26. On that morning Mr. Lincoln's coffin was lying in state at the State House in Albany, New York.

In a sense Booth died as he had lived. His life had been in the make-believe world of the theatre. His crime was agonizingly real, but he planned for it as an actor would in preparing a role for the stage. And his dying words were pure melodrama, as though he were acting out a deathbed scene in some second-rate play.

As soon as Booth was dead he was sewn into a horse blanket and carried in a wagon to Belle Plain. Herold, guarded by two soldiers, rode next to the wagon, still babbling of his innocence. The dead conspirator and the live one were brought aboard the steamer *John S. Ide* and transported to Alexandria. From there a tug took them to the Washington Navy Yard, where they were transferred to the ironclad monitor vessel *Montauk*.

*The Baker cousins pretend to dump Booth's body into the
Anacostia River*

Next morning an autopsy on Booth aboard the *Montauk* revealed "the third, fourth, and fifth cervical vertebrae and a portion of the spinal cord perforated by a conoidal pistol ball, fired at a distance of a few yards." Several people came on the *Montauk* to identify the body. Booth's appearance had greatly altered. His mustache had been shaved off at Dr. Mudd's, but now his face was covered with an eleven-day growth of beard. Exposure and hunger had shriveled and yellowed his features.

Yet on the back of his hand was his well-known tattoo "J. W. B." The dentist who had filled Booth's teeth only a few weeks before recognized the fillings. The doctor who had recently removed a large fibroid tumor from the back of Booth's neck identified the incision scar. No doubt about it: the dead body was that of the actor John Wilkes Booth.

What to do with that body? Detective L. P. Baker, who had been in on the search for Booth and the kill, and his cousin, Chief Detective L. C. Baker, thought up a scheme to prevent any grisly mishandling of the corpse. While a big crowd on the Navy Yard shore watched, the two lowered the body from the *Montauk* into a small boat. With the help of two soldiers, they rowed down the Anacostia River toward the Potomac. Still barely in sight of the observers, they began their ruse. Noisily handling a big ball and chain, they pretended to weight the corpse with it and to throw the chain-encumbered body into the river.

Drifting out of view, they then rowed across the mouth of the Anacostia to the Old Penitentiary, located on the Arsenal grounds. They brought the body ashore and into the building. There they unlocked an ammunition storage room. Using a gun-case for a coffin, they buried Booth beneath the floor. Then they tiptoed out, locking the door behind them.

(Booth's body remained in this hiding place for four years. All that time his mother and his brother Edwin besieged President Johnson to let them have the remains. Finally they were permitted to remove the body for burial in an unmarked gravesite in the family plot in Baltimore.)

Now the roundup of suspects was complete: one dead, eight living. Paine, Atzerodt, Spangler, Herold, O'Laughlin, and Arnold were imprisoned in the holds of the two monitors, *Saugus* and *Montauk*. Dr. Mudd was held in Carroll Prison, and Mrs. Surratt in the Old Capitol Prison. The U.S. government was ready to put them on trial.

President Andrew Johnson signed an executive order directing that a special military commission of nine officers be speedily chosen to try the accused. Normally the prisoners would have been tried before a civil court. A military court was used only where civil courts were not functioning. But Attorney General James Speed, backed by Secretary of War Stanton, had decided that a military, rather than a civil, trial was in order.

Speed's reasoning was that the commander in chief of the nation's armed forces had been slain at a time when the country was still at war (all the Confederate armies had not yet surrendered). The murder had taken place in Washington, D.C., a city at least in part under military rule.

A probable reason for the haste in convening the court was this: At this very time, the U.S. Supreme Court was considering the case of Milligan, an Indiana civilian, who had already been tried and convicted by a military commission in a place where civilian courts were in session. If the Supreme Court

Mudd is captured in hold of Steamer Thomas A. Scott

Secretary of War Edwin M. Stanton

ruled for Milligan, the conspirators' military trial would have been out of order. The Supreme Court later did decide that such trials were unconstitutional. But the decision came too late to do the conspirators any good.

Chosen to preside at the trial was Major General David Hunter, an old personal friend of the late President. Another on the commission was Major General Lew Wallace, who later wrote the long-time best-selling novel *Ben Hur*. Prosecuting officers were Brigadier General Joseph Holt, the Army's Judge Advocate General; Special Judge Advocate John A. Bingham, a Congressman from Ohio; and Brigadier General Henry L. Burnett. The trial officers, handpicked by Stanton, set up their own procedural rules. One important one was that a two-thirds vote was enough for conviction. Unanimity was not necessary.

On the night of April 29, the prisoners were moved to the Old Penitentiary (where Booth already lay buried). Mrs. Surratt was heavily veiled; the men wore suffocating canvas hoods over their heads and shoulders. The eight were lodged in cells on the second and third floors. Each occupied cell had an empty cell on either side, and each prisoner was guarded by four soldiers. Mrs. Surratt's feet were chained together. The men wore stiff shackles and steel anklets linked by chains to an iron ball for each foot.

The prisoners did not have many days to wait. Trial began on May 9 — five days after President Lincoln had been buried at Springfield, Illinois.

Broken columns: a symbolic portrait of the conspirators

9
THE SLATE WIPED CLEAN

Secretary of War Edwin M. Stanton had taken command the night Mr. Lincoln was shot, and he remained in command through the trial of the eight conspirators. He was a far more powerful figure than the new President, Andrew Johnson. Stanton was a hard-driving, emotion-ridden man. Once the suspects were in his hands he was determined to see them punished. And it did not matter whether the fine points of the law or of justice were observed.

A great man had been murdered, and everyone connected with his death had to pay for the crime — that was the way Stanton figured. Nor did he want to stop with the eight already captured. He was convinced that top Southern leaders, even Confederate President Jefferson Davis himself, were involved in the slaying.

The Military Commission: Col. D. R. Glendenin, Col. C. H. Tompkins, Brig. Gen. T. M. Harris, Brig. Gen. A. D. Howe, Brig. Gen. James A. Ekin, Maj. Gen. Lew Wallace, Maj. Gen. David Hunter, Maj. Gen. A. V. Kautz, Brig. Gen. R. S. Foster, Special Judge Advocate John A. Bingham, Assistant Judge Advocate H. L. Burnett, Judge Advocate General Joseph Holt

Stanton also believed that the Confederate officials had planned to spread deadly germs, start fires, and poison the water supplies in large Northern cities. They had schemed, Stanton was sure, to set off explosions in Union ships and starve Northern prisoners of war to death. He accused the South of planning "the disorganization of the North by infernal plots."

Most historians agree that Stanton's charges set the stage for his political group, the Radical Republicans, to impose a harsh postwar punishment on the South. It was the Radical Republicans who impeached President Johnson for his moderate policies in 1868 and came within one Senate vote of convicting him.

But in May 1865 Jeff Davis and the other Confederate leaders were still beyond Stanton's reach. He did have the eight accused — and he was ready to make them pay.

When the military commission convened on May 9, none of the eight had yet been permitted to choose a lawyer. Court adjourned for a single day to allow them to find counsel. The eight were comparatively fortunate. Able attorneys offered their services free of charge. They volunteered to help even though there was literally no time to prepare a defense. The lawyers could not even talk to their clients in their cells. The only place to confer was in the jammed courtroom, with the soldier-guards hovering over them. Among the defense attorneys was Reverdy Johnson, Attorney General under President Zachary Taylor and U.S. Senator from Maryland, who acted for Mrs. Surratt. The others had similarly distinguished reputations.

Trial lasted until the end of June, and more than four hundred witnesses were heard. Each day the

In courtroom, prisoners were hooded and chained

eight were brought from their cells to the raised dock in the courtroom. The men's hoods were removed, but Mrs. Surratt continued to wear her veil. Their leg irons were never taken off, and the guards had to carry the heavy balls chained to the men's legs as they walked from cell to courtroom. But none of the eight ever took the stand. Stanton saw to that.

O'Laughlin and Arnold evoked some sympathy from the spectators because of their youthful and pleasant appearances. Spangler, looking both surly and terrified, by contrast had a repellent appearance. So did Atzerodt and Herold. The spectators were not impressed by Dr. Mudd, who seemed negative, washed-out. Mrs. Surratt, veiled, sat silent, a little apart from the seven accused men. But whenever her daughter Annie visited her in her cell, the two sobbed and wept together.

Lewis Paine fascinated everyone. A black-haired giant of a young man, even his true identity was clouded. His real name may have been Powell, and he may have been the son of a Baptist minister in Florida. No friend or relative ever visited him in his cell, and he kept himself under rigid control in the courtroom. He was the only one of the eight who slept soundly at night.

Most of the prosecution witnesses were personally chosen by Stanton. He was building a wall of damning testimony, and each witness added a brick or two to that wall. Nor were the eight accused the only ones on trial. Booth, dead for weeks now, was also being tried, and the witnesses testified against him as though he were in the courtroom.

The defense attorneys did their best to break down the prosecution's attack. For example, a prosecution witness testified that he had seen Dr. Mudd in Washington the day before President Lincoln's Second

Inaugural and had in fact shown him to Booth's hotel room. To combat this story, the defense produced Dr. Mudd's sister Mary. She swore that her brother was home on his farm all that day. But, said Mary, he was wearing his "drab slouch hat"— the same hat the prosecution witness claimed Dr. Mudd was wearing in Washington that day.

Paine's lawyer, Colonel William Doster, tried a new gambit. He wanted to have Paine declared insane, hoping that the commission would not condemn a crazy man to death. Calling an insanity expert to the witness stand, Doster asked him about Paine's cry of "I am mad!" on rushing from the Seward mansion. He also asked about Paine's subsequent hiding in the trees for three days. Didn't these indicate madness? The expert said that hiding in the trees was a near-insane act. But shouting "I am mad!" was not. No madman ever admits to his madness, the expert claimed.

Mrs. Surratt was already indirectly linked with the assassination conspiracy. This was because of her son John's connection with the plotters, who often met at her boardinghouse. Two prosecution witnesses gave damaging testimony to bring Mrs. Surratt directly into the crime. John Lloyd, the tavern-keeper at Surrattsville, was one. He swore that Mrs. Surratt had left the carbines, whiskey, and field glass with him to be picked up by Booth and Herold on their flight from Washington. Louis Weichmann, the boarder, was the other. He claimed he had driven Mrs. Surratt to the tavern on that fatal Good Friday afternoon when she had deposited those articles.

By June 29 the trial was over. The courtroom was cleared of everyone except the nine-member commission and the three prosecutors who were to act

*Samuel Arnold—
Wallace sketch*

*Michael O'Laughlin—
Wallace sketch*

George Atzerodt—
Wallace sketch

Dr. Samuel Mudd—
Wallace sketch

Edman Spangler—
Wallace sketch

Lewis Paine—
Wallace sketch

Mrs. Mary Surratt—
Wallace sketch

as advisers. The fate of the eight accused was soon decided.

"Guilty!" was the verdict for all eight defendants. Spangler was sentenced to six years at hard labor. Dr. Mudd, Arnold, and O'Laughlin were given life sentences at hard labor. Paine, Herold, Atzerodt, and Mrs. Surratt were to die by hanging. The commission, however, recommended mercy for Mrs. Surratt, saying that her sentence should be commuted to life imprisonment.

(As for Mrs. Surratt's son John, he remained in hiding in Montreal, Canada. On September 15, 1865, he boarded a ship for England. He was recognized several times in Europe, but evaded capture. After two years he was caught and returned to Washington. Tried before a civil court, he admitted taking part in plans to kidnap Mr. Lincoln, but denied any role in the murder. The jury could not agree on a verdict, and John Surratt was allowed to go free.)

For days the prisoners remained ignorant of the verdict. They were confined to their cells, their heads in the hot canvas hoods, their legs shackled. Reason: President Johnson was ill and so not able to review the sentences and sign the execution orders.

Finally on July 5 he had Judge Advocate General Holt summarize the findings for him, and he signed the orders. President Johnson forever after claimed that Holt had never shown him the mercy recommendation for Mrs. Surratt. And forever after Holt claimed that the President had read the recommendation and had turned it down. Johnson, he said, reasoned that if such women were to go free, male criminals would have women commit their murders and neither would be punished.

(But as one of his last official acts before leaving office in 1869, President Johnson pardoned Arnold,

The nooses are fixed

The four are hanged

Spangler, and Dr. Mudd. O'Laughlin had already died in prison.)

Those who were to die heard their sentences on the morning of July 6. The executions were to take place "by proper military authority under the direction of the Secretary of War on the 7th of July between 10 A.M. and 2 P.M. on that day." The four had about twenty-four hours to live. Mrs. Surratt was in tears, Herold and Atzerodt were bewildered, Paine showed no emotion.

Carpenters from the Arsenal went to work in the prison yard on a gallows, and soldiers began digging graves next to it. Clergymen prayed with the condemned prisoners. Annie Surratt begged to see President Johnson, hoping for some reprieve, but she was refused. She spent the night with her mother in the cell. Herold's mother and five of his sisters stayed with him until the end was near. Atzerodt's old German mother cried over him. Only Paine remained alone, aloof, silent.

On the morning of July 7, a hot, sunny day, the gallows was finished and tested. A hundred tickets had been issued to civilian observers, and most arrived early. Thousands more clustered outside the prison walls, hoping for a glimpse of the grim proceedings. They were frustrated; soldiers patrolling the walls prevented any self-appointed witnesses from sneaking a look at the executions.

Just before 2 P.M. the condemned persons were escorted from their cells to the prison yard. Mrs. Surratt came first, led by two priests and surrounded by four soldier-guards. She resolutely mounted the thirteen steps to the gallows. She was followed by the three male prisoners, each with his own array of guards. Paine, silent no more, thanked his guards, then said unexpectedly, "Mrs. Surratt is innocent.

She doesn't deserve to die with the rest of us."

Others had believed the same, and President Johnson had been beseiged with pleas to commute her sentence until the very last minute. So distinguished a person as Mrs. Stephen A. Douglas, widow of Mr. Lincoln's old political foe, was among the pleaders. But President Johnson remained adamant, and time was running out. The execution order was read to the four condemned, and their arms and legs were bound. White hoods were put over their heads and the nooses fixed on their necks.

Adjusting the noose around Paine's neck, executioner Christian Rath, in an attempt to be merciful, told him, "I want you to die quick." Paine responded, "You know best." Mrs. Surratt cried out from under her white hood, "Don't let me fall!" Herold was silent, but his whole body trembled. And Atzerodt called to the others, "Good-bye, gentlemen. May we all meet in the next world!"

On signal, posts supporting the platform on which the four stood were knocked away, the platform swung down on its hinges — and the four fell swiftly until their nooses jerked them up. The necks of three were broken instantly. But Paine's neck muscles were strong enough to withstand the fall, and he was strangled to death by the noose.

The dead persons were allowed to hang for half an hour, then were cut down. Hoods still over their heads, they were buried in the graves dug beside the gallows.

It was all over. Justice had been served.

The murder weapon

Epilogue: The Lincoln Legend

The deaths of President Abraham Lincoln and President John F. Kennedy present many curious parallels. Some of them are nothing more than startling coincidences. Among these are:

• President Lincoln was elected in 1860, President Kennedy in 1960. Since 1840, Presidents elected in years ending in zero have met sudden, violent, or mysterious deaths.

• Mr. Lincoln and Mr. Kennedy were each succeeded by a Vice-President named Johnson.

• Each was assassinated in a public place with his wife by his side.

• Each assassin was himself killed, surrounded by police or soldiers, before he could be brought to trial.

• In turn, each assassin's slayer died before he could be punished.

And many more coincidences of the same nature. People cluck over the coincidences, but they have no significance.

Another, far more meaningful parallel is this: Was the murder of each President part of a giant conspiracy, extending far beyond the plottings of the slain assassin?

That question continues to be raised about the death of John F. Kennedy. The Warren Commission report denies that anyone but Lee Harvey Oswald was involved in the slaying. But many researchers, retracing the commission's investigations, have challenged this conclusion. None of the researchers possesses any definitive, documented proof of a conspiracy. Several, however, offer interesting — but highly circumstantial — evidence that there was more to President Kennedy's murder than first meets the eye.

Nor has there been any real case for the charge of a conspiracy surrounding President Lincoln's death. Several questions remain, however, questions that upset the neat, logical story of crime and punishment told in most history books. Among these questions:

1. President Lincoln had asked the physically powerful Major Thomas T. Eckert of the War Department Telegraph Office to accompany him to Ford's Theatre on that fatal night. The President was refused because Eckert was supposed to have had "important duties" (see p. 30). But Eckert that same night left the office early and went home to bed. Why?

2. John F. Parker, Lincoln's guard who so criminally neglected his duty (see p. 50), was never tried or punished. Why?

3. No real effort was made to track down John Surratt until long after the others were tried and convicted (*see p.* 119). Why?

4. John Lloyd and Louis Weichmann were involved in passing arms and whiskey to the fleeing Booth and Herold (*see p.* 115). They were never punished. Why?

5. Samuel Cox, Thomas Jones, William J. Jett, (*see pp.* 88-89, 94-96) and others who knowingly helped Booth and Herold on their flight were questioned and allowed to go free. Why?

6. Yet Dr. Samuel Mudd, whose aid to the fugitives was no greater than that of the others, (*see p.* 88) was punished severely. Why?

And so on.

These disturbing questions, like similar ones asked about the Kennedy assassination, in all likelihood will never be answered. There will always be a mystery surrounding the death of Abraham Lincoln — a mystery on its way to becoming a myth. For the life and death of Abraham Lincoln have already become a legend. The account in this book — completely factual, true to recorded history — is nevertheless part of that legend.

ABRAHAM LINCOLN
1809 - 1865